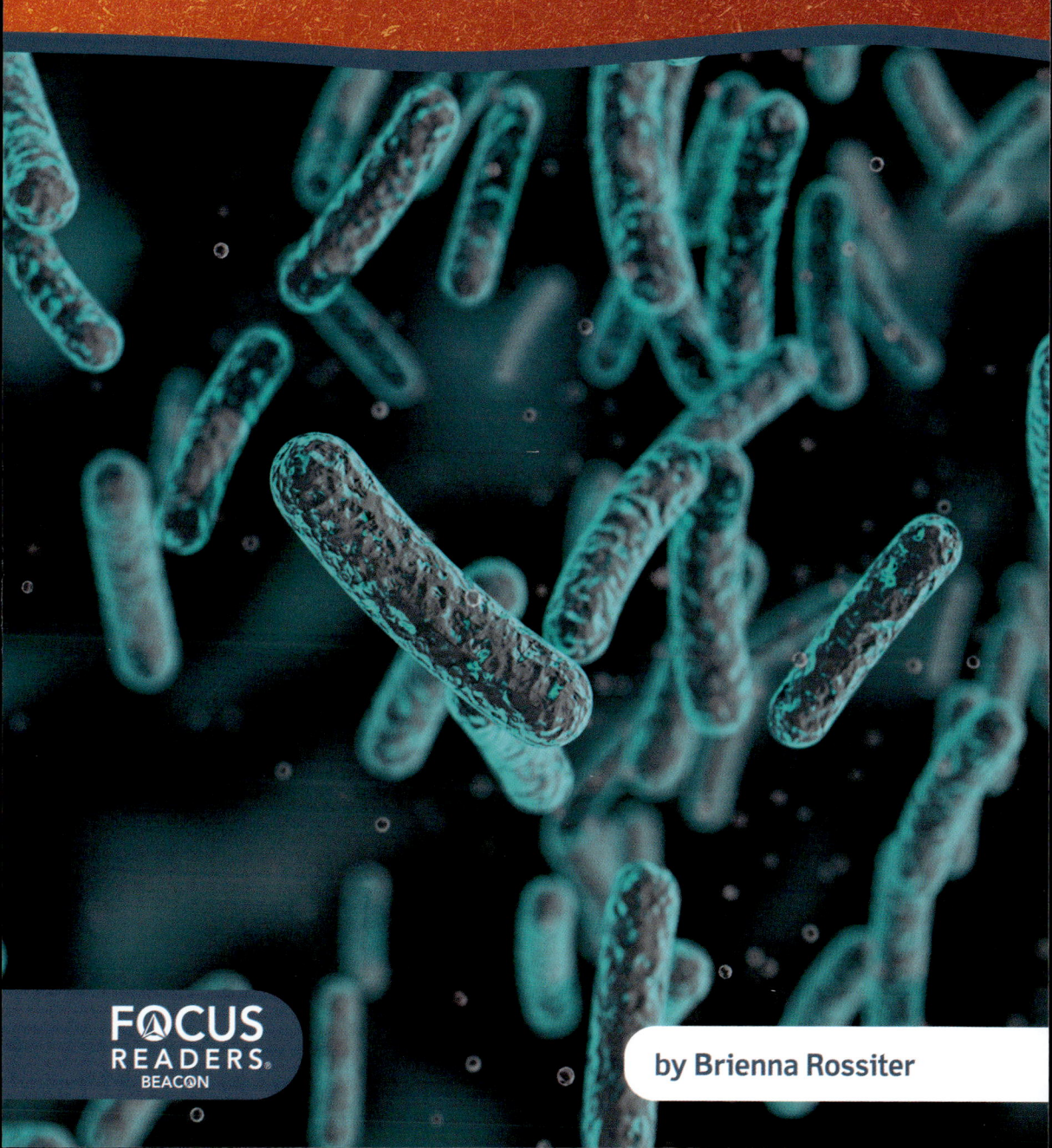

DECOMPOSERS

Bacteria

by Brienna Rossiter

FOCUS READERS®

BEACON

www.focusreaders.com

Focus Readers is distributed by North Star Editions:
sales@northstareditions.com | 888-417-0195

Produced for Focus Readers by Red Line Editorial.

Photographs ©: Shutterstock Images, cover, 1, 6, 8, 11, 12, 18, 21, 22, 24, 26, 29; iStockphoto, 4, 14, 17

Library of Congress Cataloging-in-Publication Data
Names: Rossiter, Brienna, author.
Title: Bacteria / Brienna Rossiter.
Description: Mendota Heights, MN: Focus Readers, [2025] | Series:
  Decomposers | Includes bibliographical references and index. | Audience:
  Grades 2-3
Identifiers: LCCN 2024024599 (print) | LCCN 2024024600 (ebook) | ISBN
  9798889983972 (hardcover) | ISBN 9798889984252 (paperback) | ISBN
  9798889984795 (ebook pdf) | ISBN 9798889984535 (hosted ebook)
Subjects: LCSH: Bacteria--Juvenile literature.
Classification: LCC QR74.8 .R677 2025 (print) | LCC QR74.8 (ebook) | DDC
  579.3--dc23/eng/20240606
LC record available at https://lccn.loc.gov/2024024599
LC ebook record available at https://lccn.loc.gov/2024024600

Printed in the United States of America
Mankato, MN
012025

About the Author

Brienna Rossiter is a writer and editor who lives in Minnesota.

Table of Contents

CHAPTER 1

Cleaning Water

Dirty water enters a treatment plant. Screens filter out rocks, dirt, and leaves. Then the water enters a tank. There, tiny particles settle to the bottom. They form a thick goop called sludge.

 **People have used bacteria to clean wastewater for more than 100 years.**

The sludge is full of bacteria and **organic matter**. The bacteria help break down the matter. Meanwhile, the water flows to a new tank. Air is added. So is more sludge. This sludge contains helpful bacteria. They eat more organic matter.

Leftover sludge drops to the tank's bottom. Cleaner water at the top flows away. This water is cleaned once more to remove leftover bacteria. It's ready to be used again.

Did You Know?

Chemicals can clean water, too. But they can harm nature. Bacteria are often safer to use.

CHAPTER 2

Reusing Nutrients

Bacteria are tiny living things. Each bacterium has just one **cell**. Most bacteria are too small to see. People often think of bacteria as germs. It's true that certain types of bacteria can cause illnesses.

 **People need microscopes to see bacteria.**

But thousands of types of bacteria exist. Many are not harmful. In fact, they play key roles in **ecosystems**.

Bacteria are part of many **food webs**. Food webs start with producers. Producers make their own food. Most plants are producers. Consumers come next. They get energy by eating other living things. Some consumers eat plants. Rabbits are one example. Others, such as hawks, eat small animals. Decomposers are the third

part of food webs. They get energy from breaking things down.

Most bacteria are decomposers. Bacteria break down dead animals. They decompose dead plants, too.

Plants need nitrogen and phosphorus. Bacteria help put these things back into the soil.

Bacteria even break down animal waste. Bacteria do this by letting out chemicals. These chemicals break the matter into small bits. Bacteria take these parts back into themselves. Often, those bits can be used again by other living things.

Bacteria free nutrients from the dead matter, too. The nutrients go back into the ecosystem. Plants and animals can use the nutrients. This process is called nutrient cycling.

Did You Know?

Some bacteria are producers. Similar to plants, these bacteria can get energy from sunlight.

CHAPTER 3

Breaking It Down

Bacteria live almost everywhere on Earth. All bacteria need moisture. So, they are common in water. But they also live in soil or air. In all these places, bacteria often play important roles.

 **Most bacteria grow best in warm, wet places.**

By eating dead things, bacteria keep them from piling up. Bacteria also free helpful chemicals for other living things. For example, plants can't use dead leaves. But bacteria can break down the leaves. The bacteria then let out chemicals and nutrients. One chemical is carbon dioxide. Plants use this chemical to grow and live.

Many bacteria can form helpful relationships with animals and plants. Some bacteria can grow on

plant roots. They help the plants take in nutrients. In return, the plants share energy with the bacteria. Other types of bacteria live inside animals' bodies. They are often part of the **digestive system**.

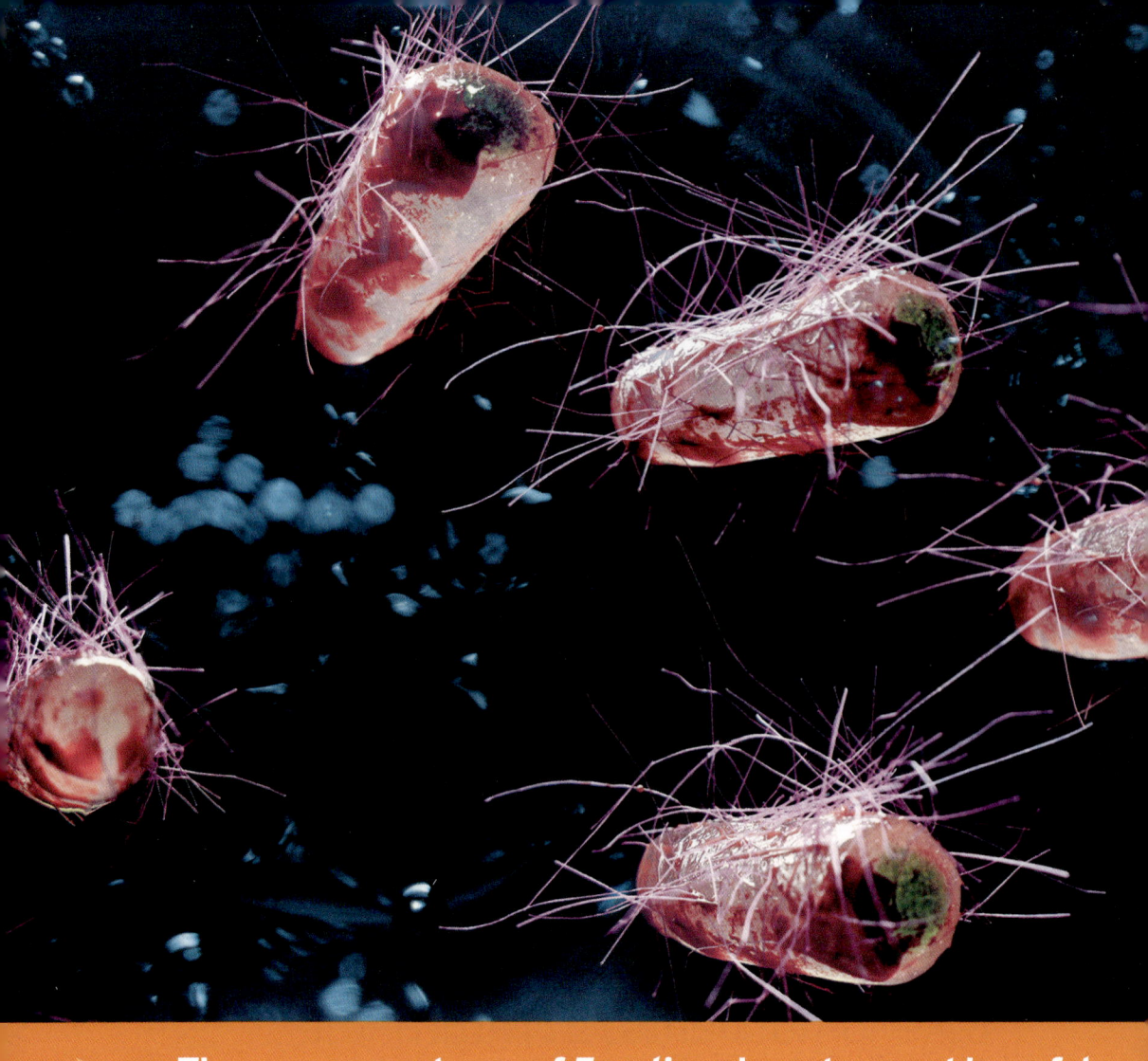

E. coli is one example. This bacteria

lives in people's intestines. It helps

break down food. But some kinds

can cause sickness if they spread outside the body.

Without bacteria, plants and animals could not survive. However, ecosystems need the right balance of bacteria. If there are too many bacteria, they use up nutrients. Or they can add too many chemicals to an area.

Did You Know?

A person's body has more bacteria cells than human cells.

Changing Traits

People don't know how many types of bacteria exist. Scientists have found more than 30,000 kinds. But some types are hard to find in the wild. Telling bacteria apart can be tricky as well. Bacteria have a few ways to change their **DNA**. Also, they can change to survive in new places. So, bacteria in the same group can look or act quite different.

In addition, some bacteria form **biofilms**. One film can contain several kinds of bacteria. They join together. This can make them hard to tell apart.

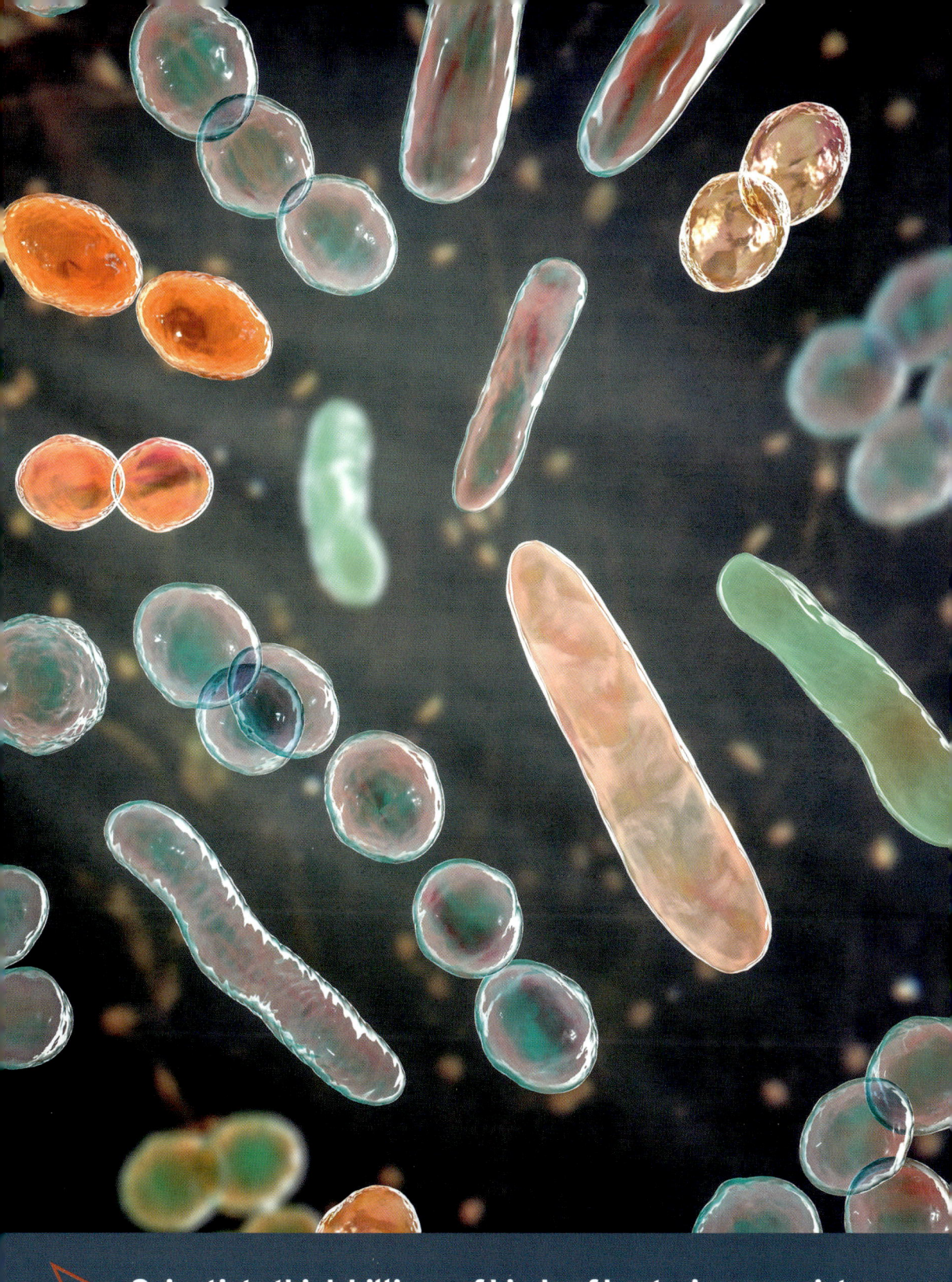

 Scientists think billions of kinds of bacteria may exist.

CHAPTER 4

Cleanup Crew

Many bacteria can break down substances that hurt other living things. For example, some types clean waste from water. Others remove harmful metals from soil.

 **Bacteria can live in places that are very warm or very cold.**

Bacteria can break oil down into carbon dioxide and water.

Bacteria can also live where other living things can't.

Bacteria often help decrease pollution. Some bacteria break down **fossil fuels**. People use these bacteria to clean up oil spills. Bacteria can also remove **pesticides** from the ground.

Some bacteria can even break down plastic. In 2001, scientists discovered bacteria that could eat PET. That is a common type of plastic. Scientists studied the bacteria. They learned how it broke down the plastic. They also found other types of bacteria that can eat plastic.

Plastic pollution is a major problem. But bacteria can help.

A company in France uses them to recycle plastic. Other ideas are being tested, too. One idea uses bacteria to break down plastic in oceans.

However, this work is just starting. Adding bacteria to ecosystems is risky. Adding too much could cause problems. So could using the wrong types. Plus, scientists may change bacteria's DNA. The changes could help bacteria break things down faster. Scientists need to do more testing to make sure the new types are safe.

Did You Know?

On its own, plastic takes hundreds of years to break down.

Focus Questions

Write your answers on a separate piece of paper.

1. Write a sentence describing one way bacteria help ecosystems.

2. Which trait of bacteria do you think is most useful? Why?

3. What type of living thing makes its own food?
- **A.** producer
- **B.** consumer
- **C.** decomposer

4. What might happen if someone had too much or too little bacteria in their intestines?
- **A.** They might get very sick.
- **B.** They might feel much better.
- **C.** They might not feel any different.

5. What does **moisture** mean in this book?

*All bacteria need **moisture**. So, they are common in water.*

   A. wetness

   B. dryness

   C. bright sunlight

6. What does **risky** mean in this book?

*Adding bacteria to ecosystems is **risky**. Adding too much could cause problems. So could using the wrong types.*

   A. totally safe

   B. possibly unsafe

   C. too expensive

Answer key on page 32.

Glossary

biofilms
Layers of bacteria that stick to the surface of something.

cell
The smallest unit of a living organism that can function and perform tasks.

digestive system
The body parts that break down food into energy and nutrients.

DNA
The genetic material in the cells of living organisms.

ecosystems
The collections of living things in different natural areas.

food webs
The feeding relationships among different living things.

fossil fuels
Energy sources that come from the remains of plants and animals that died long ago.

organic matter
Material that comes from a living thing, such as a plant or animal.

pesticides
Chemicals that kill unwanted plants or animals.

To Learn More

BOOKS

Huddleston, Emma. *Decomposers and Scavengers: Nature's Recyclers*. Minneapolis: Abdo Publishing, 2020.

Petersen, Christine. *Study Soils*. Minneapolis: Abdo Publishing, 2020.

Rosenberg, Pam. *Gross Stuff Underwater*. Mankato, MN: The Child's World, 2021.

NOTE TO EDUCATORS

Visit **www.focusreaders.com** to find lesson plans, activities, links, and other resources related to this title.

Index